Another Prayer before the Rosary

O Mary,
pray with us,
pray for us,
as we know and feel you do.

In the Rosary,
we are privileged
to share our sentiments,
words, and actions
with you
and with Your Divine Son.

May each Rosary soften
our human pains.

May it give us a taste
of the peace of the other world.

May it be our hope
of eternal life.
Amen.

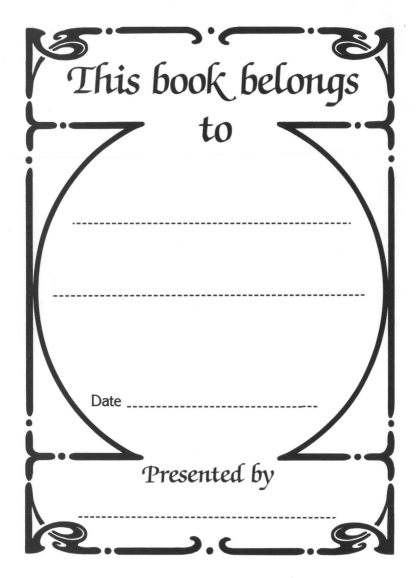

This book belongs to

Date --------------------------------

Presented by

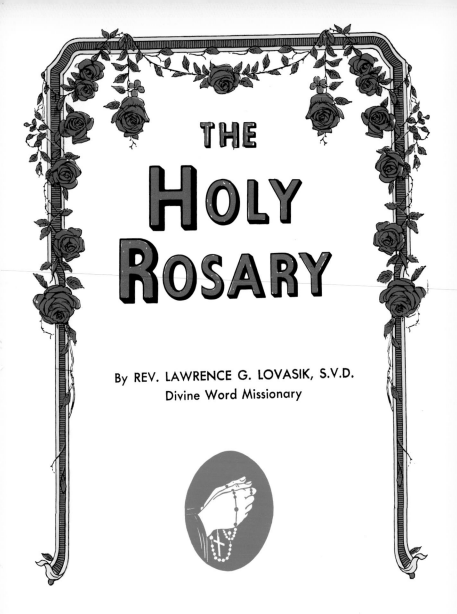

THE HOLY ROSARY

By REV. LAWRENCE G. LOVASIK, S.V.D.
Divine Word Missionary

NIHIL OBSTAT: Daniel V. Flynn, J.C.D., *Censor Librorum*
IMPRIMATUR: Joseph T. O'Keefe, *Vicar General, Archdiocese of New York*
© 1980 by *Catholic Book Publishing Co. N.Y.*—*Printed in Hong Kong*

The STORY of the HOLY ROSARY

THE devotion of the Holy Rosary has been treasured in the Church for many centuries. It is a summary of Christian faith in language and prayers inspired by the Bible. The Rosary is one of the best prayers in common that Christian families are invited to recite.

The following THREE appearances of the Blessed Virgin Mary with the Rosary will show you how much she loves that devotion.

SAINT DOMINIC

THE origin of this devotion is traditionally connected with St. Dominic who was in Spain in the thirteenth century. He founded the Order of Preachers, or Dominicans. He went to France as a missionary to convert some people.

One day the Blessed Virgin Mary appeared to

Dominic, holding a Rosary in her hand. She told him that the devotion of the Rosary would convert sinners and obtain great graces from God. She said, **"This is the precious gift which I leave to you."**

Saint Dominic taught the people how to say the Rosary. Soon, more than one hundred thousand people were converted.

OUR LADY OF LOURDES

IN 1858 the Blessed Virgin Mary appeared eighteen times to Saint Bernadette, a humble peasant girl, at Lourdes in France. She appeared in a rocky cave in a glow of brightest light. She wore a white robe and a blue sash, and on each of her feet there was a golden rose. A white Rosary with a cross of gold hung from her right arm.

The beautiful Lady said the Rosary with Bernadette. She asked her little friend to tell the people to do penance for their sins and to pray. One day Bernadette asked, "My Lady, would you be so kind as to tell me who you are?"

The Lady joined her hands and, looking up to heaven, said, **"I am the Immaculate Conception."**

Many miracles still take place at Lourdes where people say the Rosary to obtain help from the Blessed Virgin.

———

OUR LADY OF FATIMA

ON May 13, 1917, the Blessed Virgin appeared to three little shepherd children at Fatima, in Portugal. Their names were Lucy, Jacinta and Francisco. The beautiful Lady was dressed in white, and she stood on a bright cloud over a small oak tree. From her right hand hung a white Rosary. She said to the children: "Have no fear. I come from heaven. I want you children to come here on the thirteenth day of each month, until October. Then I will tell you who I am."

O N October 13, 1917, the Blessed Virgin Mary again appeared to the children of Fatima. She said: **"I am the Lady of the Rosary.** I have come to warn the faithful to amend their lives and ask pardon for their sins. People must not continue to offend our Lord, already so deeply offended. **They must say the Rosary."**

THE HOLY ROSARY

THE Rosary calls to mind the most important events in the lives of Jesus and Mary. These events are called Mysteries and are divided into three groups or decades. They are:

The Joyful Mysteries — pages 9 to 14.
The Sorrowful Mysteries — pages 15 to 20.
The Glorious Mysteries — pages 21 to 26.

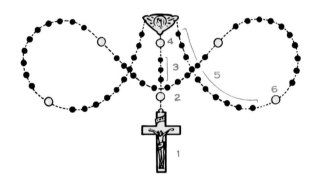

HOW TO SAY THE ROSARY

1. Begin on the crucifix and say the Apostles' Creed.
2. On the 1st bead, say 1 Our Father.
3. On the next 3 beads, say Hail Mary.
4. Next say 1 Glory Be. Then announce and think of the first Mystery and say 1 Our Father.
5. Say 10 Hail Marys and 1 Glory be to the Father.
6. Announce the second Mystery and continue in the same way until each of the five Mysteries of the selected group or decades is said.

THE PRAYERS OF THE ROSARY

THE SIGN OF THE CROSS

IN THE NAME of the Father, and of the Son, and of the Holy Spirit. Amen.

THE APOSTLES' CREED

I BELIEVE in God, the Father Almighty, Creator of heaven and earth; and in Jesus Christ, His only Son, our Lord; Who was conceived by the Holy Spirit, born of the Virgin Mary, suffered under Pontius Pilate, was crucified, died and was buried. He descended into hell; the third day He rose again from the dead; He ascended into heaven, and sits at the right hand of God, the Father Almighty; from thence He shall come to judge the living and the dead.

I believe in the Holy Spirit, the Holy Catholic Church, the communion of saints, the forgiveness of sins, the resurrection of the body, and life everlasting. Amen.

THE OUR FATHER

OUR Father, Who art in heaven, hallowed be Thy name; Thy kingdom come; Thy will be done on earth as it is in heaven. Give us this day our daily bread; and forgive us our trespasses as we forgive those who trespass against us; and lead us not into temptation, but deliver us from evil. Amen.

THE HAIL MARY

HAIL Mary, full of grace! the Lord is with thee; blessed art thou among women, and blessed is the fruit of thy womb, Jesus. Holy Mary, Mother of God, pray for us sinners now and at the hour of our death. Amen.

THE GLORY BE TO THE FATHER

GLORY be to the Father, and to the Son, and to the Holy Spirit. As it was in the beginning, is now, and ever shall be, world without end. Amen.

The FIVE JOYFUL Mysteries

The **Joyful Mysteries** help us to think of Mary's joy when Jesus came into the world. They are:

1. The Annunciation
2. The Visitation
3. The Birth of the Child Jesus
4. The Presentation of Jesus in the Temple
5. Finding of Jesus in the Temple

(Usually said on Mondays, Thursdays, the Sundays of Advent, and Sundays from Epiphany until Lent.)

THE ANNUNCIATION

MARY, my Mother, I love you as I see you telling the angel that you are ready to become the Mother of God because this is the Will of the Heavenly Father.

Thank Jesus for wanting to become a child for love of me. Make me humble and obedient that I may always please God as you did.

Say 1 Our Father. 10 Hail Marys. 1 Glory be.

THE VISITATION

MARY, my Mother, I love you as I see you making a long journey to visit and help your cousin Elizabeth before the birth of Saint John.

Teach me to be kind to people as you always were and to help them in every way I can.

Say 1 Our Father. 10 Hail Marys. 1 Glory be.

THE BIRTH OF THE CHILD JESUS

MARY, my Mother, I thank you for giving us a Savior in Bethlehem. He was born for love of us to give us the graces we need to be good and to save our souls.

Thank Him for His love. Help me to love Jesus as you loved Him, that I may save my soul.

Say 1 Our Father.
10 Hail Marys.
1 Glory be.

12

4th JOYFUL MYSTERY
THE PRESENTATION OF JESUS IN THE TEMPLE

MARY, my Mother, I thank you for offering Jesus to the Heavenly Father when you brought Him to the Temple in Jerusalem forty days after His birth.

Offer Jesus to the Heavenly Father for me that He may forgive my sins.

Say 1 Our Father. 10 Hail Marys. 1 Glory be.

5th JOYFUL MYSTERY

FINDING OF JESUS IN THE TEMPLE

MARY, my Mother, I love you as I see you looking for Jesus for three days and finding Him among the teachers in the Temple.

I want to obey you as Jesus did. Never let me lose Jesus by sin. If I should hurt God by sin, give me true sorrow and bring Jesus back to my heart at once.

Say 1 Our Father. 10 Hail Marys. 1 Glory be.

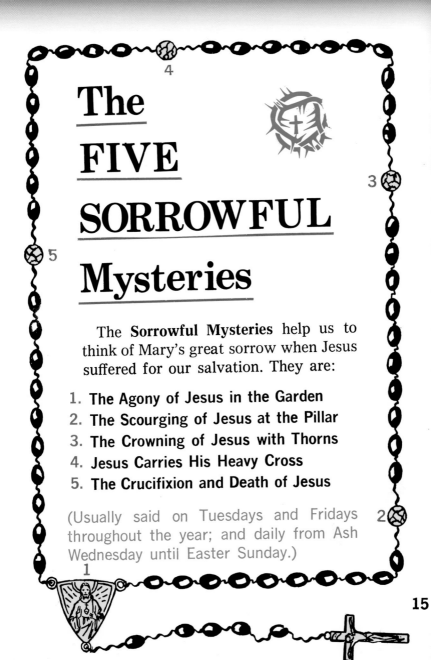

The FIVE SORROWFUL Mysteries

The **Sorrowful Mysteries** help us to think of Mary's great sorrow when Jesus suffered for our salvation. They are:

1. **The Agony of Jesus in the Garden**
2. **The Scourging of Jesus at the Pillar**
3. **The Crowning of Jesus with Thorns**
4. **Jesus Carries His Heavy Cross**
5. **The Crucifixion and Death of Jesus**

(Usually said on Tuesdays and Fridays throughout the year; and daily from Ash Wednesday until Easter Sunday.)

1st SORROWFUL MYSTERY

THE AGONY OF JESUS IN THE GARDEN

MARY, dear Mother of Sorrows, I thank you for all you have suffered with Jesus for love of me when in agony He sweat blood as He saw my sins.

Give me true sorrow for my sins, which have hurt Jesus so much.

Say 1 Our Father. 10 Hail Marys. 1 Glory be.

THE SCOURGING OF JESUS AT THE PILLAR

MARY, dear Mother of Sorrows, I thank you for all you have suffered with Jesus for love of me when He was scourged by the soldiers until His body was torn with wounds.

Let me never hurt Jesus by any evil word or deed. I beg you to keep my body pure and my soul holy.

Say
1 Our Father.
10 Hail Mary.s.
1 Glory be.

17

3rd SORROWFUL MYSTERY
THE CROWNING OF JESUS WITH THORNS

MARY, dear Mother of Sorrows, I thank you for all you have suffered with Jesus for love of me when Pilate's soldiers forced a crown of sharp thorns upon His head, struck Him, and laughed at Him.

Help me never to hurt Jesus by bad thoughts.

Say 1 Our Father.
10 Hail Marys.
1 Glory be.

4th SORROWFUL MYSTERY

JESUS CARRIES HIS HEAVY CROSS

MARY, dear Mother of Sorrows, I thank you for all you have suffered with Jesus for love of me when you met Him carrying His cross to Calvary. You saw Jesus fall three times beneath the heavy cross.

Help me to carry cheerfully every cross which God may send me.

Say 1 Our Father.
10 Hail Marys.
1 Glory be.

THE CRUCIFIXION AND DEATH OF JESUS

MARY, dear Mother of Sorrows, I thank you for all you have suffered with Jesus for love of me when you saw the soldiers nail His hands and feet to the cross, and when you saw Him die to save my soul.

Let me never hurt Jesus by any evil action, but help me to serve Him all my life that I may save my soul.

Say 1 Our Father.
10 Hail Marys.
1 Glory be.

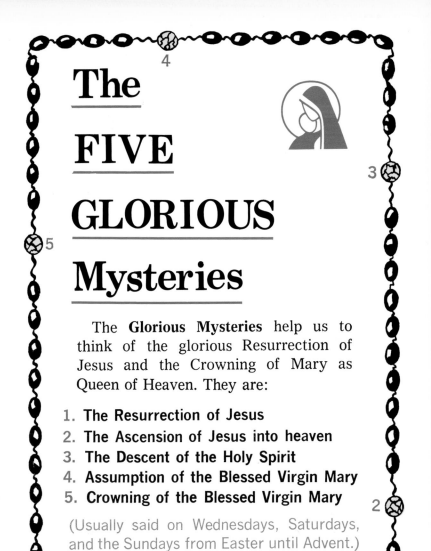

The FIVE GLORIOUS Mysteries

The **Glorious Mysteries** help us to think of the glorious Resurrection of Jesus and the Crowning of Mary as Queen of Heaven. They are:

1. The Resurrection of Jesus
2. The Ascension of Jesus into heaven
3. The Descent of the Holy Spirit
4. Assumption of the Blessed Virgin Mary
5. Crowning of the Blessed Virgin Mary

(Usually said on Wednesdays, Saturdays, and the Sundays from Easter until Advent.)

21

1st GLORIOUS MYSTERY
THE RESURRECTION OF JESUS

MARY, lovely Queen of Heaven, I love you for the joy you felt when Jesus arose from the grave in glory and showed Himself to you.

Help me to love Jesus with a love like yours on earth, that I may be happy with Him and you in heaven.

Say 1 Our Father.
10 Hail Marys.
1 Glory be.

22

2nd GLORIOUS MYSTERY
THE ASCENSION OF JESUS INTO HEAVEN

MARY, lovely Queen of Heaven, I love you for the joy you felt when you saw Jesus ascend into heaven forty days after His Resurrection.

Never let my heart look for the joys of this world, but for the true joys of heaven.

Say 1 Our Father.
10 Hail Marys.
1 Glory be.

23

3rd GLORIOUS MYSTERY

THE DESCENT OF THE HOLY SPIRIT

MARY, Queen of Heaven, I love you for the joy you felt when, on the tenth day after His Ascension, Jesus sent the Holy Spirit upon you and the disciples who were praying in Jerusalem.

I ask the Holy Spirit to visit me with His grace and to make me holy.

Say 1 Our Father.
10 Hail Marys.
1 Glory be.

4th GLORIOUS MYSTERY

ASSUMPTION OF THE BLESSED VIRGIN MARY

MARY, lovely Queen of Heaven, I love you for the joy you felt when you were taken to heaven, body and soul, by the angels.

Pray for me, a sinner, now and at the hour of my death, that I may die happily in your arms.

Say 1 Our Father.
10 Hail Marys.
1 Glory be.

5th GLORIOUS MYSTERY
CROWNING OF THE BLESSED VIRGIN MARY

MARY, lovely Queen of Heaven, I love you for the joy you felt when you were crowned Queen of Heaven and earth by the Blessed Trinity.

From the throne of your glory look upon me, your loving child, and keep me ever under your mantle so that I may one day join Jesus and you in heaven.

Say 1 Our Father.
10 Hail Marys.
1 Glory be.

26

OTHER PRAYERS TO THE BLESSED VIRGIN MARY

After the Rosary

HAIL, HOLY QUEEN

HAIL, Holy Queen, Mother of mercy, our life, our sweetness and our hope; to you do we cry, poor banished children of Eve; to you do we send up our sighs, mourning and weeping in this vale of tears. Turn, then, most gracious advocate, your eyes of mercy toward us, and after this our exile show unto us the blessed fruit of your womb, Jesus. O clement, O loving, O sweet Virgin Mary!

℣. Pray for us, O holy Mother of God.

℞. That we may be made worthy of the promises of Christ.

Let us pray

O GOD, whose only-begotten Son, by His life, death and resurrection, has purchased for us the rewards of eternal life; grant, we ask You, that, meditating upon these mysteries of the Most Holy Rosary of the Blessed Virgin Mary, we may imitate what they contain and obtain what they promise, through the same Christ our Lord. Amen.

THE MEMORARE

REMEMBER, O most gracious Virgin Mary, that never was it known that anyone who fled to your protection, implored your help or sought your intercession, was left unaided. Inspired with this confidence, I fly to you, O Virgin of virgins, my Mother. To you I come, before you I stand, sinful and sorrowful. O Mother of the Word Incarnate, despise not my petitions, but in your mercy hear and answer me. Amen.

CONSECRATION TO MARY

HOLIEST Virgin, with all my heart I praise you above all the angels and saints in paradise as the Daughter of the Eternal Father, and to you I consecrate my soul and all its powers. Hail Mary . . . .

Holiest Virgin, with all my heart I praise you above all the angels and saints in paradise as the Mother of the only-begotten Son, and to you I consecrate my body with all its senses. Hail Mary . . . .

Holiest Virgin, with all my heart I praise you above all the angels and saints in paradise as the Bride of the Holy Spirit, and to you I consecrate my heart and all its affections, praying you to obtain for me from the Ever-Blessed Trinity all the graces which I need for my salvation. Hail Mary . . . .

LITANY OF THE BLESSED VIRGIN MARY

LORD, have mercy.
Christ, have mercy.
Lord, have mercy.

Christ, hear us.
Christ, graciously hear us.

God the Father of Heaven, have mercy on us.

God the Son, Redeemer of the world, have mercy on us.

God the Holy Spirit, have mercy on us.

Holy Trinity, one God, have mercy on us.

Holy Mary,*

Holy Mother of God,
Holy Virgin of virgins,
Mother of Christ,
Mother of Divine grace,
Mother most pure,
Mother most chaste,
Mother inviolate,
Mother undefiled,

Mother most amiable,
Mother most admirable,
Mother of good counsel,
Mother of our Creator,
Mother of our Savior,
Virgin most prudent,
Virgin most venerable,
Virgin most renowned,
Virgin most powerful,
Virgin most merciful,
Virgin most faithful,
Mirror of justice,
Seat of wisdom,
Cause of our joy,
Spiritual vessel,
Vessel of honor,
Singular vessel of devotion,
Mystical rose,
Tower of David,
Tower of ivory,
House of gold
Ark of the covenant,
Gate of heaven,
Morning star,

* Pray for us.

29

Health of the sick,
Refuge of sinners,
Comforter of the afflicted,
Help of Christians,
Queen of Angels,
Queen of Patriarchs,
Queen of Prophets,
Queen of Apostles,
Queen of Martyrs,
Queen of Confessors,
Queen of Virgins,
Queen of all Saints,
Queen conceived without original sin,
Queen assumed into heaven,
Queen of the most holy Rosary,

Queen of Peace,
Lamb of God Who take away the sins of the world, spare us, O Lord.
Lamb of God, Who take away the sins of the world, hear us, O Lord.
Lamb of God, Who take away the sins of the world, graciously hear us, O Lord.

℣. Pray for us, O holy Mother of God.

℟. That we may be made worthy of the promises of Christ.

Let us pray

GRANT, we beg You, O Lord God, that we Your servants may rejoice in continual health of mind and body; and through the glorious intercession of Blessed Mary ever Virgin, be freed from present sorrow and enjoy eternal gladness. Through Christ our Lord. Amen.

ROSARY NOVENA PRAYER
For a special favor

HOLY Virgin Mary, Mother of God and our Mother, accept this Holy Rosary which I offer you to show my love for you and my firm confidence in your powerful intercession. I offer it as an act of faith in the mysteries of the Incarnation and Redemption, as an act of thanksgiving to God for all his love for me and all mankind, as an act of atonement for the sins of the world especially my own, as an act of petition to God through your intercession for all the needs of God's people on earth, but especially for this earnest request.

(Mention your request.)

I beg you, dear Mother of God, present my petition to Jesus, your Son. I know that you want me to seek God's will in my request. If what I ask for should not be God's will, pray that I may receive that which will be of greater benefit for my soul. I put all my confidence in you.

MARY, STAR OF THE SEA

HAIL, brightest Star of ocean,
  God's own Mother blest,
Ever-sinless Virgin,
Gate of heavenly rest!

Virgin all excelling,
Mildest of the mild,
Freed from guilt, preserve us
Meek and undefiled.

Keep our life all spotless,
Make our way secure,
Till we find in Jesus
Joy forevermore.

Through the highest heaven
To the Almighty Three,
Father, Son and Spirit,
One same glory be. Amen.

Other Great Books for Children

FIRST MASS BOOK—Ideal Children's Mass Book with all the official Mass prayers. Colored illustrations of the Mass and the Life of Christ. Confession and Communion Prayers.   Ask for No. 808

The STORY OF JESUS—By Father Lovasik, S.V.D. A large-format book with magnificent full colored pictures for young readers to enjoy and learn about the life of Jesus. Each story is told in simple and direct words.   Ask for No. 535

CATHOLIC PICTURE BIBLE—By Rev. L. Lovasik, S.V.D. Thrilling, inspiring and educational for all ages. Over 110 Bible stories retold in simple words, and illustrated in full color.   Ask for No. 435

LIVES OF THE SAINTS—New Revised Edition. Short life of a Saint and prayer for every day of the year. Over 50 illustrations. Ideal for daily meditation and private study.   Ask for No. 870

PICTURE BOOK OF SAINTS—By Rev. L. Lovasik, S.V.D. Illustrated lives of the Saints in full color. It clearly depicts the lives of over 100 popular Saints in word and picture.   Ask for No. 235

Saint Joseph CHILDREN'S MISSAL—This new beautiful Children's Missal, illustrated throughout in full color. Includes official Responses by the people. An ideal gift for First Holy Communion.
Ask for No. 806

St. Joseph FIRST CHILDREN'S BIBLE—By Father Lovasik, S.V.D. Over 50 of the best-loved stories of the Bible retold for children. Each story is written in clear and simple language and illustrated by an attractive and superbly inspiring illustration. A perfect book for introducing very young children to the Bible.   Ask for No. 135

WHEREVER CATHOLIC BOOKS ARE SOLD

Prayer after the Rosary

O God,
by His Life, Death, and
Resurrection,
Your only Son Jesus
purchased for us
the rewards of eternal life.

Grant that,
by thinking about these
Mysteries
of the Most Holy Rosary
of the Blessed Virgin Mary,
I may imitate
what they contain
and obtain
what they promise.

I ask this
through Christ our Lord.
Amen.